Page Turners

Gone

Julian Thomlinson

Series Editors:
Rob Waring and Sue Leather
Series Story Consultant: Julian Thomlinson
Story Editor: Sue Leather

NATIONAL GEOGRAPHIC LEARNING | CENGAGE Learning®

Australia • Brazil • Japan • Korea • Mexico • Singapore • Spain • United Kingdom • United States

NATIONAL GEOGRAPHIC LEARNING | CENGAGE Learning

Page Turners Reading Library

Gone

Julian Thomlinson

Publisher: Andrew Robinson

Executive Editor: Sean Bermingham

Editorial Assistant: Dylan Mitchell

Director of Global Marketing: Ian Martin

Senior Content Project Manager: Tan Jin Hock

Manufacturing Planner: Mary Beth Hennebury

Contributor: Vessela Gasper

Layout Design and Illustrations: Redbean Design Pte Ltd

Cover Illustration: Eric Foenander

Photo Credits:

43 Anton Gvozdikov/Shutterstock
44 nimon/Shutterstock
45 topten22photo/Shutterstock

ISBN-13: 978-1-4240-4873-1

ISBN-10: 1-4240-4873-7

National Geographic Learning
20 Channel Center Street
Boston, Massachusetts 02210
USA

Cengage Learning is a leading provider of customized learning solutions with office locations around the globe, including Singapore, the United Kingdom, Australia, Mexico, Brazil, and Japan. Locate your local office at:
international.cengage.com/region

Cengage Learning products are represented in Canada by Nelson Education, Ltd.

Visit National Geographic Learning online at **NGL.Cengage.com**

Visit our corporate website at **www.cengage.com**

Printed in the United States of America
1 2 3 4 5 6 7 – 18 17 16 15 14

Contents

Review

Background Reading

People in the story

Ricky Robson
an Englishman in his
early thirties

Anna Robson
Ricky's wife, also in her
early thirties

Aik
a mysterious Thai lawyer
and businessman

Officer Boomsa
a Thai police officer

The story is set on the island of Koh Samui, a very popular tourist destination in the south of Thailand.

£1 (British Pound) = approximately 53 THB (Thai Baht)
(exchange rate in 2014)

Chapter 1

The sea

The plan was simple. Rent a small boat from Fisherman's Village, go out to one of the islands, eat on the beach, swim in the sea, and be back at the hotel by four o'clock. Just as they did the first time.

It all started out just fine. Sure, the boat was a bit more expensive than last time—it was ten years after all—but £60 for a day's boat rental was still cheap, and Captain Jeet seemed like a nice guy. As they set off in the boat, Ricky started to feel as though they were going to have a good day. Just maybe, after three days of problems and things going wrong, today they were going to enjoy themselves.

No more than twenty minutes after he had this thought, it started to rain. Ricky couldn't believe it. He checked the weather twice—once last night and again this morning—and it was supposed to be sunny all day. It was just a little rain at first, but then the sky turned dark, the wind got stronger, and the boat started going up and down in the water. Ricky felt sick.

"Are you all right?" Anna asked. "You look a bit green."

"Fine, fine," Ricky said. After all the trouble of the last few years, after all the money they saved to come back to Samui, he didn't want to go back to the hotel just because of a bit of rain. He went up to see Captain Jeet and make sure everything was OK.

"It's not good," Jeet said. He pointed to the west, where the sky was almost black. "That's where we're going. You don't want to eat your lunch in that, do you?"

"Can we not try another island?"

"Too far," Jeet replied.

"Oh, let's just try," Ricky said. "I mean, the rain could just pass over us, right?"

"Maybe," said Jeet. He didn't seem happy about it. "If it gets worse, we're going back."

"What was that about?" Anna asked, when Ricky sat back down.

"Oh, he wants to go back," Ricky said. "He says the weather could get worse."

"Oh, no!" Anna said.

"I said let's keep going," Ricky said. He put his arm around his wife. "Let's see. It could get better, right?"

It got worse. The rain came down hard, and big waves started hitting the boat. At one point Ricky thought the boat was going over, but it was Jeet turning them around. Ricky got up to talk to him, but Anna put a hand on his arm.

"It's all right," she said.

"It's not all right!" Ricky said.

This was the story of the whole holiday. Everything was going wrong. Their favorite restaurant was closed. The hotel made a mistake with the room, and they had to spend the first two nights in a room at the back. It looked out onto a wall and smelled of fish. Then Anna lost her bag. Now there was this.

Was it just bad luck? Ricky wasn't sure. It seemed to him the whole island was different. There were more people. It wasn't as friendly. Even the sea wasn't as clear as it used to be. When they first came, ten years ago, it seemed like the best place in the world. A place where nothing could ever go wrong. That's why they came here again—to try and forget the last few difficult years, and remember how happy they used to be. Except that wasn't happening.

It was as if the weather was just there to stop them from having a good time, because back at Fisherman's Village it was sunny. He could feel people looking at them as they stepped off the boat, tired and wet and unhappy. Ricky asked Jeet for some of the money back—they paid for a full day and it was only eleven o'clock—but the boat captain said no. By the time they got to the hotel, Ricky was in a terrible mood.

"I can't believe we had to pay for the whole day," Ricky was saying. "Next time, I'm not going to pay anything until later. And what about the weather? Can you believe it's not even raining here?"

"Ricky, please just stop," Anna said.

"Stop what?" Ricky asked.

"Everything!" Anna said, almost shouting. Anna never shouted.

For a moment neither of them spoke, then Ricky said, "What's wrong?"

Anna sat down on the bed. "Could you just give me a few minutes? To myself?"

"Are you OK?"

"I'm fine," she said, turning away from him. "Please, Ricky."

"Maybe I'll take a shower," Ricky said. "Are you sure you're OK?"

"I'm sure," she said. "Go. Have a shower."

Ricky went into the bathroom and turned on the shower, but he could still hear Anna in the next room. She was crying.

Chapter 2

Strangers

He wanted to go back and speak to her, but thought maybe it was a good idea to leave her for a while. He got in the shower and thought about what to do. Why was Anna so upset with him? Things weren't working out like they had hoped, but he wasn't getting angry with her for it.

"Hey, Anna," he shouted through the door. "We're not having much luck, are we?"

There was no reply. Ricky knew he wasn't helping, getting angry about everything. What was it his dad always said? Getting angry about things only makes them worse.

"Hey, Anna, I'm sorry," he said, stepping out of the shower. "How about if we go to that Italian restaurant tonight? You know the one I mean?"

Still nothing. Ricky put his shorts on and went back into the bedroom. Anna wasn't there. For a moment he thought she was playing a joke on him, because he didn't hear her go out. But she wasn't in the room—that was for sure.

"Anna?" he said, checking the balcony. She wasn't there either. *Maybe she's just gone to the shop or something*, Ricky thought. He was just going back inside when something on the street caught his eye. A man and a woman were walking up the street together. They were quite far away, but the woman looked just like Anna. She was wearing a

black T-shirt and shorts, like Anna sometimes wore, and she had long blonde hair, just like Anna. She even walked like Anna. The guy with her was very tall. He had long, dark hair and was wearing a pair of red shorts. They were talking as they walked, turning their heads to each other. Were they arguing? It was so strange. It felt as though he was watching Anna in a movie, playing a different person.

The man put his hand on the woman's arm, as if trying to stop her. She pulled it away and carried on walking. The man stopped, watching her go, then turned and walked the other way. Then the woman walked behind a big building and he couldn't see her any more. *She looked so much like Anna,* Ricky thought. He went back inside and tried calling her, but her phone was turned off. No answer. He took out a book and lay on the bed with it, trying to read. An hour passed, but still no Anna. He sent her an email—maybe she was at an Internet café—and sat at his computer waiting for a reply. Soon he couldn't wait any more, so he went down to see if he could find her.

Nobody in the hotel knew where she was, so Ricky went down to the beach and looked in the cafés and restaurants there. Anna wasn't in any of them. He came back to the road and looked in the shops and the big hotels with expensive cars out front, but she wasn't in any of those either. Two hours went by like this, walking around, getting hot and tired. *Maybe she's taken a taxi somewhere,* he thought. He didn't think so, at least not without her phone. He went back to the hotel to see if she was there, but she wasn't. He took another shower to cool down and think, then went back to all the shops and cafés, this time with Anna's picture. He showed everyone the picture of Anna on his phone, but nobody knew her. It was getting dark when he went in the motorbike rental shop. Anna didn't ride a motorbike, but he wanted to try everywhere. The woman was closing up, pushing a bike off the street.

"Closing, sir," she said, going into her office. Ricky followed her inside.

"You want to rent a motorbike?" she asked him.

"I'm looking for my wife," Ricky said, holding up the picture of Anna on his phone. The woman looked at it.

"Oh, I don't know," she said.

"Please take a good look," Ricky said.

"Many people come in," she said, taking a box from under the desk. It was full of passports of people who have rented motorbikes. "I'm not sure."

"Have another look, would you?" Ricky said. "Maybe she passed by sometime this afternoon."

"I don't think so," the woman said. She started taking the passports out of the box and putting them in a safe. "I don't know. I'm sorry."

"I understand," Ricky said. "Thanks a lot." He was just about to leave when something stopped him. One of the passports was in a pink holder, just like Anna's.

"Wait a second," he said. "Can I see that?" He showed her what he meant. She opened the passport to the photo page and Ricky's heart jumped—he was looking at a picture of his wife.

"That's my wife's passport!" he told her. "Anna Robson."

"Oh, yes," said the woman, checking a piece of paper in the passport. "She came in today . . . just before one o'clock. Sorry."

"What did she want?" Ricky asked. The woman looked at him strangely.

"She wanted to rent a motorbike," she said.

She wanted to what?

"She doesn't ride a motorbike," Ricky said.

"Oh," the woman said. She seemed surprised, but didn't say anything else about it.

"How long did she rent it for?" Ricky asked.

"She paid for one day," the woman said.

"Can you remember anything else?" Ricky asked.

The woman thought about it for a few moments.

"Sorry, no, I can't," she said.

"Did she say where she was going?"

"Sorry, I wish I could help more, but . . ."

Ricky thanked her and went back out onto the street. *Anna rented a bike?* As far as he knew, Anna didn't even know how to ride a motorbike. What did she want a motorbike for? Where was she going?

He went back to the hotel to think about it, but by now it was dark and Ricky really began to worry. Soon it was ten o'clock, then eleven. He kept telling himself that any minute Anna would walk in the door, but she didn't. Ricky knew then, knew really strongly: Anna wasn't coming back.

Chapter 3

Police

The closest police station was in Chaweng town, about fifteen minutes from the hotel in a taxi. There were three officers at the desk and a few Thais in the waiting room, but most of the people in there were foreign. One of the Thais, a hard-looking man around forty or so, smiled at Ricky as he went in. Ricky didn't like the look of him at all. He went to the other side of the room and introduced himself to one of the officers, Officer Boomsa. Ricky told him how Anna left the hotel around twelve o'clock and didn't come back. He told him she rented a motorbike, and that he thought she was in trouble. The policeman didn't reply.

"I'm sorry," Ricky said. "Did I speak too fast? Should I start again?"

"Come back tomorrow," Officer Boomsa said after a few moments.

He doesn't understand my English, Ricky thought. He began again, much more slowly. "My wife . . . Anna Robson . . ."

"Yes, yes, I understand," Boomsa said. "But it's only been a few hours."

"Twelve hours," Ricky said. "She went out at about twelve o'clock."

"Twelve hours, maybe, yes," said Boomsa, looking at his watch. "Maybe she fell asleep on the beach. Maybe she

met some friends. This kind of thing happens all the time. It's too early to say she's a missing person. It has to be twenty-four hours."

"But you don't understand," Ricky said and the policeman's eyes went cold. "Anna's never done anything like this before."

"I see."

"The thing is," Ricky went on, "I absolutely know she wouldn't stay out without telling me. She just wouldn't."

Boomsa took a deep breath. "OK. She went out about lunch time, you say."

"That's right, yes," said Ricky. "It was just after twelve."

"Did she say where she was going?" Boomsa asked.

"No, she didn't."

"She didn't say? Did you ask?"

"No," said Ricky. "It wasn't like . . . The thing is, she was kind of angry."

"She was angry?" Boomsa said. "Why? Did you have a fight?"

"No, we didn't have a fight. I didn't say we had a fight."

"What did you fight about?" Boomsa asked. Something made Ricky turn around and he noticed the hard-looking man was still watching him.

"We didn't fight. It was just . . . one of those things. When you've been married for ten years . . ." Ricky told him. "You understand, right?"

"Oh, I understand," Boomsa said. "Come back tomorrow."'

Ricky sat down in front of a restaurant and tried to decide what to do. It was easy to be angry with Officer Boomsa, but he knew it was like this everywhere. Twelve hours wasn't long enough to report someone missing. It didn't matter that *he* knew that something was wrong. He thought about the motorbike again . . . and the woman with blonde hair he saw from the balcony. Before, he was *sure* it wasn't Anna. Now he wondered.

Ricky knew there was something he should do, something that could help him find her, but he was so worried he couldn't think what that was. Suddenly a shadow came over him and he looked up to see the hard-looking Thai man from the police station. The man wasn't tall or big, but he was harder-looking up close. Ricky didn't like the look of him at all. He was sure more trouble was coming his way, but then the man spoke in a low, soft voice.

"Let me guess, Brother," the man said. "You've lost your wife, haven't you?"

Chapter 4

Aik

Ricky thought he heard him wrong and asked, "What did you say?"

"I said I think you've lost your wife," the man said. "Is that right? It's right, isn't it?"

"I don't think it's any of your business," Ricky said, standing up. "If you know something, you'd better tell me what it is."

"Ah, I'm sorry," the man said, putting up his hands. "I didn't mean it like that. My name's Aik." He put his hand out. Ricky wasn't sure what else he could do so he took it. With his other hand, Aik passed Ricky a card. It said:

"Mongkol Petcharong (Aik). Lawyer, businessman, language teacher. Your friend in Thailand."

Ricky wasn't sure about the "friend" bit. Aik was still talking.

"It's just that people get a certain kind of look on their face when someone goes missing. You've got that look now. Now your wedding ring tells me it's a wife or a child, but if it's a child . . . then you would be here with your wife as well."

That's all I need, Ricky thought. *The Sherlock Holmes of Thailand.*

"You don't look like a lawyer," Ricky said.

"What does a lawyer look like? You're talking about the clothes? It's midnight on a Friday. What should I be wearing?"

Not just the clothes, Brother, Ricky thought, but he didn't say it.

"Weren't you working?" Ricky said. "What were you doing at the police station?"

"Just helping someone," Aik said.

"Well, you must know I just spoke to the police . . ." Ricky began.

". . . and they told you to come back tomorrow," Aik finished. "Did you call the British Embassy yet?"

"Good idea," Ricky said, taking out his phone.

"Forget about it. They won't do anything. Listen. These people are busy. They're not going to help you until they're sure something's wrong. Now maybe nothing's wrong. Let's say she's had an accident. She could be in one of the hospitals. Did you check hospitals?"

The hospitals—of course, Ricky thought. She was on a motorbike, after all.

"I'm not thinking straight at all," Ricky said. "Thanks for that. Thanks a lot." He was about to start walking until he realized he didn't know where any hospitals were.

"Try and relax there," Aik said. "Listen. What's your name, Brother?"

"Ricky."

"Ricky, I've got the number of just about every hospital on the island here. I can call them or I can take you to them.

I can talk to people around the island, get them to show her picture around, see if anybody's seen her. I can talk to Thais for you. You can only speak to people who speak English. I can talk to everyone. I can do whatever you need me to do to find your wife. If anybody on this island can help you find your wife, it's me. I would even say while you have been unlucky losing your wife, you have been very lucky finding me. So what do you say?"

Aik put his hand out again. Ricky didn't trust the hard-looking lawyer (if he was a lawyer), but he didn't know what else he could do.

"How much do you cost?" he asked Aik.

"Good question," said Aik. "It depends on what we do. I can start at 6,000 Baht a day." Ricky worked it out. It was less than £120. Cheap for a lawyer, a little less than he expected even, but still the price of two nights at the hotel.

"How about 5,000?" Ricky said.

"Done," said Aik, holding his hand out again.

Ricky took it. "OK," he said. "Let's go."

Chapter 5

Anna

Aik told Ricky to wait and went to get his car. After ten minutes or so Ricky started to wonder if he was coming back, but then a big white car stopped in front of him, the door opened, and Aik waved him inside. The inside of the car was like a nightclub. There were no seats in the back; in their place was a clear box with speakers and red and blue lights inside. They were going on and off with the music. Ricky wondered what he was doing.

"I called the Samui International Hospital and the Bandon Hospital already," Aik was saying. "No foreign women have come in today. I can't get through to Thai International Hospital so let's go and see. It isn't far." He started to drive away before Ricky closed the door. "I need you to send me a picture of her. Do you have one on your phone? Send it to the number on the card I gave you. What was her name again? Your wife, I mean."

"Anna," Ricky said. "Anna Robson."

"Anna. Nice name," Aik replied. "About your age?"

"Thirty-one," Ricky told him.

"Listen," Aik began, "I need to ask you something. You probably don't want to hear it but it's important. Is there any chance she's with someone else?"

"No," Ricky said, thinking about the woman he saw from the balcony and the man with the red shorts.

"OK," said Aik. "Was there any problem between you

two? Any kind of fight? Anything that could make her want to stay out this long?"

"No," Ricky said. "She's not that kind of person."

"No problem between you?"

"Not really, no. I mean nothing really. Let's just check the hospitals."

"Brother, if you want me to help you, you've got to trust me a little bit," Aik said softly.

"I'm sure she's not with anyone," Ricky said. "She rented a motorbike."

"OK. She didn't say where she was going? Is that normal for her? Going off on a motorbike?"

"As far as I know, she's never been on a bike in her life," Ricky told him.

"That's interesting," Aik said. "But she didn't say where she was going."

Anna wasn't in the Thai International Hospital. Though there were a lot of foreigners there—everyone in the waiting room seemed to be foreign. There was even a girl who was in the hospital because she fell off a motorbike, but she was from Germany. Ricky sat in the waiting room with a coffee while Aik made one phone call after another, talking fast in Thai before hanging up.

"She isn't in any hospital," he said. "I've called every one on the island, and none of them have heard of Anna Robson. I sent her picture to some people as well. They'll call me if they see her. We need to think about some other things we can do. Anything else you can tell me?"

Ricky was thinking about the woman he saw in the street, the one that looked like Anna. He still didn't know if it was her or not, but he told Aik about it anyway. Once he started talking, he couldn't stop. He told him about all the problems they had. He told him about their arguments, about the baby they wanted, but couldn't have. He told him about how they came to Thailand to try and start again, how this was their last chance to make things work. Aik listened, quiet for once, and waited for Ricky to finish before he spoke.

"The woman in the street. Do you think it was Anna or not?" Aik said.

"I didn't at the time. Now . . . I'm just not sure."

"If she went off on a bike, maybe it makes no difference," Aik said. "We should check this out though. Did you look through her things? These black clothes you saw. Did she bring them?"

"I . . . think so," Ricky said.

"Did you check if they were still in her bag?"

"I didn't," Ricky said. "I'll do that as soon as I get back."

"If the guy was near the hotel, there's a good chance he's staying around there. What time is it?" It was just after 3 a.m. "We can't go now. It'll have to be tomorrow."

The thought of spending the rest of the night without his wife next to him, worrying about where she was, suddenly made Ricky feel like he might go crazy. He stood up.

"Is there nothing else we can do?" He was almost shouting. A few people turned to look at him. Aik put his hand on his arm.

"Go back and see if those clothes are in her bag," Aik said. "Then get some sleep."

Chapter 6

The man from yesterday

Ricky checked through Anna's things, and there were two black T-shirts, but no shorts. He took another shower, then tried to sleep, but couldn't. When it was about 6 a.m., the sun started to come into the room. He got up, made himself a cup of tea, sat out on the balcony, and drank it. *Where are you, Anna?* he thought. It was very quiet. An old woman sat with a dog out at the front of her shop. Two young men were pushing a bike up the street, laughing and talking. At the end of the street, someone was running, a tall man with long hair and red shorts.

Long hair and red shorts.

Was it the man from yesterday?

Ricky put his cup down, pulled on a T-shirt and shoes, grabbed his phone, and ran out of the room. He couldn't remember the last time he ran fast, but he had to catch the man. He jumped down the last few steps and ran fast across the hotel lobby. By the time he was outside, he was already breathing hard.

Slow down, Ricky, he said to himself. It wasn't easy. He couldn't see the man as he came out of the hotel and he didn't want to lose him. It was already hot and as Ricky ran past the bike shop he wished more than anything he had one of the motorbikes. He ran on down the street, trying to breathe steadily. The man in red shorts was in front, running easily. Ricky thought about shouting, but he was too far away. The man couldn't possibly hear him. *Better save your strength,* he thought, then, *when did I get so old?* The guy was a much better runner than he. *What if I can't catch him?* The thought made Ricky feel sick.

Suddenly the man disappeared and Ricky worried for a moment before he realized that he turned onto the beach. *That's good,* Ricky thought. *He'll go slower on the sand.* Ricky ran on until he came to the next hotel, and then cut through the garden toward the water.

The man in red shorts was still a long way away and seemed to be running well, even on the beach. The sand was soft, making it harder to run. The beach went on for another kilometer or so, but Ricky knew he couldn't go on much longer.

"Hey!" he shouted. "Hey, wait!"

The man didn't seem to hear him. *What if he's listening to music?* Ricky thought, then began to run as fast as he could. He was lucky to see the man in the first place, and he knew he had to take the chance. Slowly, he started to get closer, but his legs hurt and his chest burned. His head felt light.

"Stop," he shouted. "Stop . . . please stop!"

Again, the man didn't turn, but a Thai man on a fishing boat saw him. Ricky waved at him.

"Please," he said. It was hard to speak. "Stop him. Please."

At first it looked as though he didn't understand, but then the fisherman waved at the man in red shorts and pointed back at Ricky. Finally, the man stopped, looking around at him. Ricky was still out of breath when the runner reached him.

"Are you all right there?" the man asked. He sounded Australian. Now that he was in front of him, Ricky wasn't sure what to say.

"Wait a second," said Ricky, getting his breath back.

"You wanted to talk to me, right?" the man said.

"Yeah," Ricky replied. "Yesterday . . . I saw you . . . with a woman. She had blonde hair . . . a black T-shirt. Wait." He showed him the picture of Anna on his phone.

"Oh yeah," he said. "I saw her. Why?"

So it *was* Anna.

"What did she say to you? Do you know where she was going?"

"What's this about?"

"She's my wife," Ricky said. "She's missing."

"Oh, right," the man said. He looked worried, suddenly. "She didn't say much, really. I just asked her what was wrong. She was really upset. I asked if I could help; that was all."

Ricky took his arm.

"What did she say?"

"Relax," the man said. "I only talked to her for a minute or something."

"I'm sorry," Ricky said. "I'm just really worried about her. I just need to know where she's gone."

"Well, she was upset. I asked if she was OK. I asked if she needed help. She said no. I said, look, has something happened? Can I take you somewhere, or something? Oh, yeah, that's what she said. I forgot about that."

"What?"

"She said something really strange. She said, 'Can you take me back in time?' I thought she was a bit strange when she said that."

"Can you take me back in time?" Ricky repeated.

"That's what she said."

Ricky didn't know what to say to that.

"Listen, if that's all . . ." the man said.

Ricky was sure there were other things he should ask, but he couldn't think what they were. *Go back in time? What's that all about?*

Before he could think of anything, his phone rang. It was Aik.

"Where are you, Brother?" Aik was saying. "I'm at your hotel."

"Did you find anything?" Ricky asked.

"Yeah," Aik said. "I got a call from one of the hospitals."

"And?" Ricky said.

"You'd better come back. I don't want to say over the phone."

"Tell me!"

"It sounds like she's in one of the hospitals. Ricky, I'm sorry. It's bad news."

"What do you mean, 'bad'?"

"They found a woman on one of the beaches this morning. I gave Anna's description and they said they think it's her. It seems she went swimming in the night and . . . I'm sorry, Ricky. I'm so, so sorry."

Ricky started running.

Chapter 7

The hospital

It only took ten minutes to drive to the hospital, but it was the longest ten minutes of Ricky's life. He had no idea what to do or what would happen next. He just sat quietly and let Aik drive, wondering how it came to this. When they arrived at the hospital, Aik took his arm and led them inside where a nurse was waiting. She showed them to a large white room with a table in the middle. Looking at the body, lying there under a white cloth, Ricky found it hard to breathe. He almost fell and Aik took his arm again, as if to hold him up. A doctor came in and without a word pulled back the sheet. Ricky opened his mouth to cry out, to let out all the fear and pain that was inside him, but the face stopped him. It wasn't Anna.

"It's not her," he cried. "It's not her."

The doctor looked as though he didn't understand for a moment, then started shouting at the nurse in Thai.

"Are you sure?" Aik asked. He was looking carefully at the woman's face.

"Yes," Ricky said. "I'm sure. It looks like her, but it's not her."

Aik started shouting then. Ricky took hold of the table, to stop himself from falling. The white face of the woman on the table was the worst thing he'd ever seen, but it wasn't his wife. It wasn't Anna.

He left the three Thais and went back to Aik's truck. All he wanted to do was climb in the back, pull up his knees, and cry. But he didn't. The girl in the hospital wasn't Anna, but if they didn't find her soon . . . He couldn't think like that. They needed to find her. He went through the events in his mind, starting with the boat. He was thinking hard when Aik came back.

"I don't know what to say," Aik said. "I'm so sorry. I told them about Anna over the phone, gave her description, and the nurse said they found her. I asked her if they were sure. She said as sure as she could be."

A day or two ago, Ricky knew he would be shouting at Aik by now, getting angry about yet another thing going wrong. Instead he said, "She's not in any of the hospitals. She's not with this guy I saw her with in the street. But she was upset. She rented a motorbike. She was upset."

"She was going somewhere," Aik said.

"Yeah. You think?"

"It's the only reason to rent a bike," Aik went on. "When you have a fight with someone, you leave the room, you want to think. You don't get a bike. You get a bike if you want to go somewhere. Think, Brother. Where did she want to go?"

Ricky knew this was the question he needed to answer. Anna didn't say where she was going, just that she wanted to think. He knew what else she wanted: to be happy again. To make everything better. That's why they came back to Thailand. To remember how to be happy. To remember how to love each other. That's why they went to the same restaurants, the same places. He thought about the first time they came. It really was the best week of his life. He thought about how they took the boat around the islands, how they went swimming at night. He thought about the waterfall, how he asked her to be his wife, how she said, "Of course I will."

Can you take me back in time? she said to the man with long hair.

The waterfall.

"I'm so stupid," he said.

"What?" asked Aik.

"I know where she went," Ricky said.

Chapter 8

The decision

As they drove, Ricky told him. Ten years ago, Ricky rented a bike and drove them around the island. They didn't really know where they were going, but they found themselves on this little road, going up into hills where they found a small waterfall. There was nobody around and the sun was shining and it seemed like the most beautiful place in the world. It was there that Ricky brought out the ring he'd been carrying the whole time, waiting for the perfect moment. It was there he asked Anna to marry him.

"So why go there now?" Aik asked.

"I don't know," Ricky said. "Maybe she wanted to make a decision. Maybe she wanted to know if it was worth it. It feels right. I'm sure she's there."

"So where is it exactly?" Aik said.

"I don't know, but I think I can find it. Turn left here."

They drove for over an hour, going up and up. It was hard to see far because of all the trees. A few times Ricky realized they were going the wrong way, and they had to turn back and take a different road. It was ten years since Ricky and Anna first came, but this part of the island was the same as before. He didn't stop to ask himself if he was right or not. He trusted his feelings. After another half hour of driving, they found the waterfall.

It was just as he remembered it. Except for one thing:

Anna wasn't there.

"Let's go back," Aik said. "We can go and talk to the police again. We can try the hospitals again."

"She must be here," Ricky said. "I was so sure."

"Come on, let's go," Aik said.

They got back into his truck. It took nearly five minutes to get it turned around on the little road, but finally they got started down the hill. Ricky felt lost. He had been so sure—and so wrong. At least that's what he was thinking as they continued down the hill, until something in the grass caught his eye. Something red.

"Stop," Ricky said.

"What is it?" Aik said, stopping the car. But Ricky was already out. He noticed the long grass was broken at the side of the road, as if something big had gone through it. Then he saw it. A motorbike. And he heard the voice.

"Ricky?" it said, all weak and broken. It was Anna.

She lay on her side in the grass, her back facing the sun. Her face was bloody and one eye was closed.

"I found you," Ricky said. "Oh, I found you."

He sat down in the grass next to her. He wanted to reach out to hold her, but he stopped himself. She was hurt, and he didn't want to make her worse.

"I'm so sorry," Anna said. "I've been really stupid, haven't I?"

"Shh," Ricky said. "It'll be all right."

"Who's this, Ricky?" Anna said.

Ricky turned to find Aik standing there. Aik opened his mouth to speak, but Ricky answered for him.

"He's a friend," Ricky said.

"Hi," Anna said, trying to smile at Aik. Ricky loved her for that.

"There's some water in the truck," Aik said. "Wait a moment."

He came back with a bottle and gave it to Ricky, who helped Anna drink.

"Not too much," Aik said. "She'll probably need surgery. Her leg looks bad."

"Thanks," Anna said.

"I'm going to call the hospital," Aik said. "But I can't explain where we are. I'm going to have to go and meet them by the road and show them how to get here. Are you going to be all right?"

"We'll be fine," Ricky said, getting up. "Aik, I don't know what to say. I'm going to get you the money as soon as we . . ."

"Don't talk about that now," Aik said, then he was gone.

Ricky sat down next to Anna. He gave her another drink. The sun was high now, and it was getting hot.

"I'm sorry," Anna said again.

"Don't be," Ricky said. "I'm the one who should be sorry. I know why you came."

"Yeah?"

"To make a decision?"

"I was here for hours, thinking about the best thing to do. I didn't even notice it was dark. So I started back, but . . ." She didn't need to finish.

"It's all my fault," Ricky said.

"Ricky, I . . ."

"No, wait, Anna," Ricky said. "I want to say something. I've been so angry these last few years. Shh, you don't need to say anything; I know how I've been. I don't know how you've done it. We've had some problems, maybe, but I've just been making everything worse. I'm sorry, Anna. I'm so sorry."

"Oh, Ricky, I'm sorry, too."

"I thought I was never going to see you again," Ricky said. "We got a call from a hospital. I thought you were . . . I almost lost my mind. The idea of being without you . . . I can't do it, Anna. I just can't. I can't live without you."

"Oh, Ricky."

"I knew that if I saw you again, I wasn't going to forget. I promise, I'm never going to forget again. I know it's been hard. But I want to stay together, Anna. I know things can't be just like they were. I know things change. I know there will be problems. But I want to keep going, Anna. Isn't that all we can do? Keep going?"

"I want to, Ricky," Anna said. "I want to."

He put his arms around her then, and together they sat in the grass, holding each other. The sun was almost down, making everything gold and beautiful. At that moment Ricky felt so much love, it was like everything was made of that sunlight. *Whatever happens,* he said to himself, *I can't forget this. I will not forget this.* A light wind blew across the top of the hill. Ricky pulled his wife closer, and waited.

Review: Chapters 1–4

A. Number these events in the order they happened (1–6).

______ Ricky searches for his wife near the hotel.

______ Ricky and Anna have a fight.

______ Ricky goes to the police.

______ Ricky and Anna go on a boat trip.

______ Anna goes out of the hotel and does not return.

______ Ricky starts to worry about his wife.

B. Choose the best answer for each question.

1. Why does Ricky think the woman he sees from the hotel balcony may NOT be Anna?

a. Because she's talking to a stranger.

b. Because she doesn't walk like Anna.

c. Because he thinks Anna is still in the hotel.

2. Why is Ricky surprised that Anna rented a motorbike?

a. Because Anna hates motorbikes.

b. Because he doesn't think Anna can ride a motorbike.

c. Because he thinks he saw her walking on the street.

3. Why doesn't Officer Boomsa help Ricky more?

a. Because he doesn't like the way Ricky speaks to him.

b. Because Ricky makes him angry.

c. Because Anna hasn't been missing for very long.

4. Why does Aik offer to help Ricky?

a. Because he thinks he knows where Anna may be.

b. Because he wants to make some money.

c. Because he likes him.

Review: Chapters 5–8

A. Match the two halves of the sentences.

1. Ricky thinks that Aik ______
2. Aik asks Ricky lots of questions about ______
3. Ricky asks the tall man with long hair about ______
4. Aik gets angry with the people at the hospital talking about ______
5. Ricky talks to Anna about ______

a. Anna being in an accident.
b. what Anna said to him when they met in the street.
c. how much he loves her.
d. why Anna went out of the hotel on her own.
e. drives a very strange car.

B. Read each statement and circle whether it is true (T) or false (F).

1. When Ricky gets into Aik's car, he thinks he's lucky to find such a helpful person. T / F
2. Aik calls lots of people to try to find Anna. T / F
3. Ricky tells Aik about all the problems he and Anna had. T / F
4. Ricky gets upset and hits the tall man with long hair. T / F
5. The girl in the hospital looks like Ricky's wife. T / F
6. Aik proves to be a helpful, good person. T / F
7. Anna goes out to the waterfall because that's where Ricky asked her to marry him. T / F
8. At the end of the story, Ricky and Anna decide to end their marriage. T / F

Answer Key

Chapters 1–4

A:
5, 2, 6, 1, 3, 4

B:
1. a; **2.** b; **3.** c; **4.** b

Chapters 5–8

A:
1. e; **2.** d; **3.** b; **4.** a; **5.** c

B:
1. F; **2.** T; **3.** T; **4.** F; **5.** T; **6.** T; **7.** T; **8.** F

Background Reading:

Spotlight on . . . Staying safe while traveling

Traveling, whether in your own country or abroad, is one of the most interesting and fun things you can do. But if things go wrong, even a dream vacation can turn into a nightmare. Here are some ways to stay safe while on vacation:

- Don't look like a tourist; if you have a camera, keep it in a bag.
- Eat and drink like the locals. This is also a great way to meet new people.
- Always keep your bags with you—leaving them unattended is asking for trouble.
- Give family and friends your travel plans. If things do go wrong, you'll be glad you did.
- Learn the language; even knowing a few words in a foreign language can make a big difference in how you are treated.
- Stay on the third to fifth floor. Staying on one of these means that you'll be less likely to have something stolen, at least according to statistics.
- Be careful at night; always try to arrive by day and find your way around.
- Most of all, don't do anything you wouldn't do at home. Relaxing on a beach can make you feel like nothing bad can happen, but it can.

Think About It

1. Which of these things are the easiest/hardest to do?

2. Can you think of some more?

Spotlight on . . . *Seven things to do in Thailand*

Thailand is a beautiful country. With almost 20 million foreign visitors a year, it's one of Asia's most popular tourist destinations. But what kinds of things do people do when visiting Thailand? Here are seven of the most exciting things to do in the country often called the "Land of Smiles."

1. Go shopping. There are many great places to shop in Thailand, but the floating market in Bangkok is one of the most famous.

2. Visit temples. Thailand has some of the world's most interesting and beautiful temples. Some of the most famous are Wat Arun in Bangkok and Doi Suthep in Chiang Mai.

3. Relax on the beach. As well as Koh Samui, Thailand has a number of world-class beaches, such as those around Phuket in the Andaman Sea.

4. Go scuba-diving. There are many beautiful things to see under water as well as on the land.

5. Go on a boat ride. One of the easiest ways to get around Bangkok is by riverboat, and many of the city's best sights are close by. Some rides are as little as 8 baht—less than 30 cents!

6. Get in a water fight. During the Songkran festival, from 13 to 15 April, Thai people love to throw water over each other. If you go out at this time, you can expect to get wet!

7. Enjoy the local food! Some of the world's most delicious food can be found in Thailand. But be careful . . . a lot of it is really spicy!

Think About It

1. What would you like to do if you went to Thailand?
2. Which would be the most interesting or exciting?

Glossary

argument	(*n.*)	an angry discussion
balcony	(*n.*)	a space on the outside of a building, above the ground
breath	(*n.*)	the air that goes in and out of your lungs through your nose or mouth
breathe	(*v.*)	to draw air into your lungs, and then send it out through your nose or mouth
embassy	(*n.*)	an office representing a government in another country
foreign	(*adj.*)	from another country
lawyer	(*n.*)	a person whose job is to offer legal advice and services
motorbike/bike	(*n.*)	a bicycle with an engine
passport	(*n.*)	a document you need for traveling to foreign countries
policeman	(*n.*)	a person whose job is to uphold the law
rent	(*v.*)	to pay to use something for a period of time
sand	(*n.*)	a beach is made of this
surgery	(*n.*)	medical treatment in which a doctor must cut into a person
trust	(*v.*)	to feel that a person will help you and not do anything bad to you
upset	(*adj.*)	unhappy, worried, or disappointed
waterfall	(*n.*)	a place where water drops down from one level to another, such as from the edge of a cliff
wave	(*n.*)	a shape made by the rising and falling of water as it moves in seas or lakes